UNDERSTANDING THE VOICE OF GOD

My sheep hear my voice, and I know them, and they follow me.

John 10:27

by

Franklin N. Abazie

Understanding The Voice of God
COPYRIGHT 2017 BY Franklin N Abazie
ISBN: 978-1-945-133-45-9

All right reserved. This book or any portion thereof may not be reproduced or used in any manner whatsoever without the express written permission of the publisher, except for the use of brief quotations in a book review. All Bible quotes are from King James Version and others as noted.

Published by: F N ABAZIE PUBLISHING HOUSE- aka, Empowerment Bookstore.

That I may publish with the voice of thanksgiving and tell of all thy wondrous works.
Psalms 26:7

To order additional copies, wholesales
or booking:
Call the Church office (973-372-7518),
or Empowerment Bookstore Hotline (973-393-8518)

Worship address:
343 Sanford Avenue Newark New Jersey 07106
Administrative Head Office address:
33 Schley Street Newark New Jersey 07112
Email:pastorfranknto@yahoo.com
Website www.fnabaziehealingministries.org
Publishing House: www.fnabaziepublishinghouse.org

This book is a production of F N Abazie Publishing House.
A publication Arms of Miracle of God Ministries 2017.
First Edition

CONTENTS

THE MANDATE OF THE COMMISSION iv

ARMS OF THE COMMISSION v

INTRODUCTION vi

CHAPTER 1
1 The Voice of The Holy Spirit 1

CHAPTER 2
2 How To Hear From God 8

CHAPTER 3
3 Prayer of Salvation 30

CHAPTER 4
4 About The Author 43

THE MANDATE OF THE COMMISSION

"THE MOMENT IS DUE TO IMPACT YOUR WORLD THROUGH THE REVIVAL OF THE HEALING & MIRACLE MINISTRY OF JESUS CHRIST OF NAZARETH."

"I AM SENDING YOU TO RESTORE HEALTH UNTO THEE AND I WILL HEAL THEE OF THY WOUNDS, SAID THE LORD OF HOST."

ARMS OF THE COMMISSION

1) F N Abazie Ministries-Miracle of God Ministries (Miracle Chapel Intl)

2) F N Abazie TV Ministries: Global Television Ministry Outreach

3) F N Abazie Radio Ministries: Radio Broadcasting Outreach

4) F N Abazie Publishing House: Book Publication

5) F N Abazie Bible School: also called Word of Healing Bible School (W.O.H.B.S)

6) F N Abazie Evangelistic Ass: Miracle of God Ministries: Global Crusade

7) Empowerment Bookstore: Book distribution

8) F N Abazie Helping Hands: Meeting the help of the needy world wide

9) F N Abazie Disaster Recovery Mission: Global Disaster Recovery

10) F N Abazie Prison Ministry: Prison Ministry for all convicts "Second chance"

Some of our ministry arms are waiting the appointed time to commence.

FAVOR CONFESSION

Father thank you for making me righteous and accepted through the blood of Jesus Christ. Because of that, I am blessed and highly favored by God. I am the subject of your affection. Your favor surrounds me as a shield, and the first thing that people see around me is your favored shield. Thank you that I have favor with you and man today. All day long people go out of their way to bless me and help me. I have favor with everyone that I deal with today. Doors that were once closed are now opened for me. I receive preferential treatment, and I have special privileges, I am Gods favored child.

No good thing will he withhold from me. Because of Gods favor my enemies cannot triumph over my life. I have supernatural increase and promotion. I declare restoration to everything that the devil has stolen from my life. I have honor in the midst of my adversaries and an increase in assets, especially in real estate and expansion of territories.

Because I am highly favored by God, I experience great victories, supernatural turnarounds, and miraculous breakthrough in the midst of great impossibilities. I receive recognition, prominence, and honor. Petitions are granted to me even by ungodly authorities. Policies, rules, regulations, and laws are changed and reverse on my behalf.

I win battles that I don't even have to fight, because God fights them for me. This is the day, the set time and the designated moment for me to experience the free favor of God, that profusely and lavishly abound on my behalf in Jesus name. Amen.

INTRODUCTION

"My sheep hear my voice, and I know them, and they follow me."
John 10:27

This book *Understanding The Voice of God* is a manual for anyone who genuinely want to hear from *the Holy Spirit*. In these end time we are in an urgent *need to hear directly from God*. Often, some folks mistake *the voice* of the devil for *the voice of God*. For anyone to *truly hear* from *the throne of God*, we must genuinely be connected to the source. Despite the prophetic mantle, and power of prayer upon Elijah, he had difficulty recognizing *the voice of God*.

"And he said, Go forth, and stand upon the mount before the Lord. And, behold, the Lord passed by, and a great and strong wind rent the mountains, and brake in pieces the rocks before the Lord; but the Lord was not in the wind: and after the wind an earthquake; but the Lord was not in the earthquake; And after the earthquake a fire; but the Lord was not in the fire: and after the fire a still small voice." **1 King 19:11-12**

In this evil generation, it is with urgency that *we recognize and differentiate* with *understanding the voice of God*. We live in a wicked generation, where no one can afford to be *misdirected* by any foul spirit. Despite the understanding of Samuel the prophet, Prophet Samuel had a big problem *recognizing the voice of God*. I pray you recognize *the voice of God* in Jesus Mighty Name.

This small book is a manual for any genuine Christian seeking the face of God, in prayer, in supplication, and in thanksgiving, to receive the *free gift of the spirit of God*. It is my desire prayer that you *hear directly from God*, more especially it is my vision that you come to repentance, and become a born again believer. May God change your life the remaining days of your life *in Jesus Mighty Name*.

"And ere the lamp of God went out in the temple of the Lord, where the ark of God was, and Samuel was laid down to sleep; That the Lord called Samuel: and he answered, Here am I. And he ran unto Eli, and said, Here am I; for thou calledst me. And he said, I called not; lie down again. And he went and lay down.

And the Lord called yet again, Samuel. And Samuel arose and went to Eli, and said, Here am I; for thou didst call me. And he answered, I called not, my son; lie down again.

Now Samuel did not yet know the Lord, neither was the word of the Lord yet revealed unto him. And the Lord called Samuel again the third time. And he arose and went to Eli, and said, Here am I; for thou didst call me.

And Eli perceived that the Lord had called the child. Therefore Eli said unto Samuel, Go, lie down: and it shall be, if he call thee, that thou shalt say, Speak, Lord; for thy servant heareth.

So Samuel went and lay down in his place. And the Lord came, and stood, and called as at other times, Samuel, Samuel. Then Samuel answered, Speak; for thy servant heareth.

And the Lord said to Samuel, Behold, I will do a thing in Israel, at which both the ears of every one that heareth it shall tingle. In that day I will perform against Eli all things which I have spoken concerning his house: when I begin, I will also make an end." **1 Samuel 3:3-11**

"Give unto the Lord, O ye mighty, give unto the Lord glory and strength. Give unto the Lord the glory due unto his name; worship the Lord in the beauty of holiness. The voice of the Lord is upon the waters: the God of glory thundereth: the Lord is upon many waters. The voice of the Lord is powerful; the voice of the Lord is full of majesty. The voice of the Lord breaketh the cedars; yea, the Lord breaketh the cedars of Lebanon. He maketh them also to skip like a calf; Lebanon and Sirion like a young unicorn.

The voice of the Lord divideth the flames of fire. The voice of the Lord shaketh the wilderness; the Lord shaketh the wilderness of

Kadesh. The voice of the Lord maketh the hinds to calve, and discovereth the forests: and in his temple doth every one speak of his glory. The Lord sitteth upon the flood; yea, the Lord sitteth King forever. The Lord will give strength unto his people; the Lord will bless his people with peace." **Psalms 29**

God speaks to His people every day. It is my desire that you do not only connect to God, but hear from the Lord directly concerning your life. May this small book be of help to you.

Happy reading

HIS DESTINY WAS THE

CROSS....

HIS PURPOSE WAS

LOVE.....

HIS REASON WAS

YOU....

"And after the earthquake a fire; but the Lord was not in the fire: and after the fire a still small voice."

1 King 19:12

PRAYER OF POWER

*"If ye shall ask any thing in my name,
I will do it.."*
John 14:14

I cover my body with the blood of Jesus, in the name of Jesus.

I plead the blood of over my family, in the name of Jesus.

I reject every demonic interruption against my life in the name of Jesus.

Arise Lord God, open the gates of prosperity in the name of Jesus.

Fire of God, melt all witchcraft covens away like wax with your fire, in the name of Jesus.

Fire of God visit all witchcraft incantations with thunder, earthquake, and great noise, in the name of Jesus.

O God arise and instruct your angels to send unquenchable fire upon witchcraft habitation and shrine, in the name of Jesus.

O God arise and cause confusion in witchcraft camps assigned against me, in the name of Jesus.

Angels of God arise and slay the power of the wicked, in the name of Jesus.

Gates of Heaven refuse to carry out the instruction of witchdoctors assigned against me in the name of Jesus.

I deprogram and cancel all witchcraft prophecies by the power in the blood of Jesus, in the name of Jesus.

I decree judgment on witchcraft into the heavens, in the name of Jesus.

Fire of God, arise, and cast abominable things upon witchcraft, in the name of Jesus.

Hand of God, let the table of witchcraft becomes their snare, in the name of Jesus.

Let the eyes of the witches assigned against me be darkened, in the name of Jesus.

Let their covens become desolate so that none can dwell in them, in the name of Jesus.

Pray this prayer three hot times: Let every witchcraft powers flying against me crash land and die, in the name of Jesus.

No witch or wizard shall prosper in my environment in the name of Jesus.

Water spirits that are networking with witchcraft against me, I judge you by fire, in the name of Jesus.

Queen of heaven that is networking with witchcraft against me, I judge you by fire, in the name of Jesus.

Let the sun go down on witchcraft networks in the name of Jesus.

Let the sun smite them by day and the moon by night, in the name of Jesus.

Let the stars in their curses fight against witches and wizards in the name of Jesus.

I shut down all witchcraft buildings with the key of David, in the name of Jesus.

Father God, arise and send out your whirlwind with great pain upon the head of witchcraft, in the name of Jesus.

O Lord, arise and trample down every witchcraft coven in the name of Jesus.

Father God, arise and cause stormy wind to fall upon witchcraft powers in the name of Jesus.

Father God, arise and bring the day of disaster upon the heads of witchcraft in the name of Jesus.

I come against all enchantment of witchcraft in the name of Jesus.

I destroy every agenda of witchcraft over my family I cut you off in the name of Jesus.

Witchcraft in the waters I crush you powers in the name of Jesus.

Witchcraft agenda for my destiny, roast by fire in the name of Jesus.

Every witchcraft power assigned to convert my life to a dustbin I dislodge you in the name of Jesus.

Witchcraft powers assigned to resurrect affliction in my life, die by fire in the name of Jesus.

Every witchcraft game plan over my success I destroy you, in the name of Jesus.

Every yoke manufactured by witchcraft to attack my life catch your owner in the name of Jesus.

Every pregnancy of sorrow assigned against my breakthrough by witchcraft powers I abort you now, in the name of Jesus.

I offset every witchcraft plan set up against my life, in the name of Jesus.

I break every witchcraft imprisonment over my life in the name of Jesus.

Every witchcraft remote control against my life I block you out in the name of Jesus.

Witchcraft powers sponsoring repeated problems in my life carry your problems in the name of Jesus.

I destroy every occultist man/woman assigned against me, in the name of Jesus.

Every household witchcraft assigned to waste my life be wasted in the name of Jesus.

Witchcraft altars and priests, die in the name of Jesus.

Every yoke designed by marine powers against my life, break in the name of Jesus.

Every evil load of witchcraft go back to your sender in the name of Jesus.

Every witchcraft prayer against my life scatter, in the name of Jesus.

Every environmental witchcraft be disgraced in the name of Jesus.

I destroy every witchcraft grip upon my family in the name of Jesus.

I shatter every witchcraft initiations against my destiny in the name of Jesus.

Satanic decree over my life I cancel you now in the name of Jesus.

Witchcraft manipulations of my finances die in the name of Jesus.

Every witchcraft padlock hanging against me lock your owner in the name of Jesus.

Every witchcraft engagement over my success break in the name of Jesus.

Every ancestral witchcraft claim over my life break in the name of Jesus.

I destroy the power of stagnation and limitation in the name of Jesus.

I cut down every tree of failure in my family line, in the name of Jesus.

I destroy every pin of witchcraft in my family line, in the name of Jesus.

Every witchcraft covenant working against my life be broken in Jesus name.

Every witchcraft register bearing my name catch fire in the name of Jesus.

Every witchcraft documents written against me be consumed by fire, in the name of Jesus.

Every witchcraft informant that is observing my destiny be paralyzed, in the name of Jesus.

Every image carved against me catch fire, in the name of Jesus.

Every witchcraft authority over my destiny break in the name of Jesus.

Every tree planted against my freedom catch fire in the name of Jesus.

Every satanic road block clear away by fire in the name of Jesus.

Every witchcraft concoction inside my body melt away by fire in the name of Jesus.

I destroy every Jezebel spirit, against my life, in the name of Jesus.

Father Lord arise in your anger and pursues my pursuer, in the name of Jesus.

Every foundation of witchcraft in my family catch fire, in the name of Jesus.

I pollute the food of witchcraft powers with the blood of Jesus in the name of Jesus.

Every seat of witchcraft working against me receive the fire of God in the name of Jesus.

Let their communication system be disrupted and be destroyed in the name of Jesus.

Let their throne be dismantled by fire and by thunder of God in the name of Jesus.

I set the fire of God into their place of refuge in the name of Jesus.

Let the east wind of God pull down the strong hold of stubborn witchcraft in the name of Jesus.

I disintegrate and scatter all the network of witchcraft in the name of Jesus.

Let the transportation of witchcraft power catch fire and burn to ashes in the name of Jesus.

Every hindering forces against my life receive double confusion in the name of Jesus.

Let the weapons of the enemy turn against them in the name of Jesus.

I speak confusion into the storehouses of witchcraft and I enter in and possess my possession in the name of Jesus.

Let their altars catch fire and burn to ashes in the name of Jesus.

I use the hammer of God to destroy their padlock in the name of Jesus.

Let the traps, nets and snares of the enemy catch them unawares in the name of Jesus.

Every demonic projection against my progress backfire in the name of Jesus.

Every witchcraft burial of my destiny receive fire and be exhumed in the name of Jesus.

Every bewitchment of my life receive the Holy Ghost fire in the name of Jesus.

I destroy every forces of hell hindering my breakthrough in the Name of Jesus.

Every power of witchcraft interrupting my life, receive the fire of the Lord, in the name of Jesus.

Lord God, destroy every satanic to forces, trouble my life in the name of Jesus.

Any powers drawing my blood vomit it and die in the name of Jesus.

Every power that has tasted my blood will not stop vomiting until it confesses in the name of Jesus.

Blood of Jesus cause confusion in the stomach of witchcraft in the name of Jesus.

Thou power of witchcraft monitor die in the name of Jesus.

Let the night birds of witchcraft be massacred by the angels of God in the name of Jesus.

Witchcraft from my place of birth militating against my life die in the name of Jesus.

Every witchcraft power, be destroyed in the name of Jesus.

I overthrow any kingdom of witchcraft assigned against my life in the name of Jesus.

Let the blood of Jesus destroy every witchcraft assigned against my life in the name of Jesus.

Every witchcraft exchange of my virtues be frustrated in the name of Jesus.

I destroy every coffin of witches plotted against my life, in the Name of Jesus.

Any witchcraft power projecting into the body of an animal in order to do me harm be trapped in that body forever, in the name of Jesus.

Let every witchcraft power be covered with shame in the name of Jesus.

Every chain of inherited witchcraft in my family break in the name of Jesus.

Every wisdom of witchcraft working against me be converted to madness in the name of Jesus.

I pray, Let the imagination of witchcraft against me be neutralized in the name of Jesus.

Father God let every witchcraft decision against my life be scattered in the name of Jesus.

O God smites witchcraft powers by their cheekbones in the name of Jesus.

Every witchcraft burial of my virtues I reverse you now in the name of Jesus.

Any tongue anointed by Satan against me catch fire in the name of Jesus.

Witchcraft powers assigned against my heavens scatter in the name of Jesus.

HOW DO I RECOGNIZE THE VOICE OF GOD?

---A still small voice---

The voice of God is not a persuasive voice. Often we are confused by that persuasive compelling voice pushing us desperately to take the wrong action, or make that wrong decision. *"There is a way which seemeth right unto a man, but the end thereof are the ways of death."* **Proverb 14:12**

To *hear the voice of God,* we must be *still,* If you must *hear* from God, *you must be calm at all times. "Be still, and know that I am God: I will be exalted among the heathen, I will be exalted in the earth."* **Psalms 46:10**

God is never in a hurry. God is never desperate. This *small still voice of God is faint* and not *loud.* It *comes freely under a serene environment.* We must therefore create the conducive atmosphere that will attract *the Holy Spirit* to *come and speak to us. "And after the earthquake a fire; but the Lord was not in the fire: and after the fire a still small voice."* **1 King 19:12**

---We must have the right mindset---

Unless you have the right mindset, God will *not speak* on that matter for you. God is a *revealer of secret*. It is written, *"Then was the secret revealed unto Daniel in a night vision. Then Daniel blessed the God of heaven."* **Daniel 2:19** It is the right intention that will provoke the Holy Spirit to speak to us.

---We must pray always---

Praying constantly provokes the Holy Spirit to speak to us. If we must *hear the voice of God* we must *pray always*. We must develop a prayer life. If anyone must hear often from God, we must operate in the spirit.

---Through the written word---

If *you must recognize the voice of God*, I recommend that you *read your bible daily*. A *daily practice of reading the Holy bible* is a great *avenue to hear the voice of God* directly from *His written word*. It is written, *"All scripture is given by inspiration of God, and is profitable for doctrine, for reproof, for correction, for instruction in righteousness: That the man of God may be perfect, thoroughly furnished unto all good works."* **2 Timothy 3:16-17**

---Through your prophet---

Although there are so many fake prophets these days, but there are some chosen by God to speak to His people. *"I will raise them up a Prophet from among their brethren, like unto thee, and will put my words in his mouth; and he shall speak unto them all that I shall command him."* **Deut 18:18**

Whenever *your God given prophet is speaking a word to you from the Lord, you should be able to discern, and confirm it.* Although some fake prophet tries to fake *the word from the Lord*, you should be able to confirm *the voice of God* through your prophet. God can speak through any of these channels. Be observant, be attentive, be open, and remain steadfast in the faith.

CHAPTER 1

THE VOICE OF THE HOLY SPIRIT

"And the spirit entered into me when he spake unto me, and set me upon my feet, that I heard him that spake unto me."
Ezekiel 2:2

In this end time, we are *all desperate to hear* from *the Holy Spirit*. Unless we have received *the free gift of the Holy Spirit*, it will be *inevitable to recognize the voice of the Holy Spirit*. It is written, *"Now when they heard this, they were pricked in their heart, and said unto Peter and to the rest of the apostles, Men and brethren, what shall we do? Then Peter said unto them, Repent, and be baptized every one of you in the name of Jesus Christ for the remission of sins, and ye shall receive the gift of the Holy Ghost."* **Acts 2:37-38**

It is the *entrance of thy word* that gives light. In my own opinion, it is not easy for *the Holy Spirit* to speak to un-believers. *"For as many as are led by the Spirit of God, they are the sons of God."* **Romans 8:14**

It is written, *"The entrance of thy words giveth light; it giveth understanding unto the simple."* **Psalms 119:130**

HOW TO CONNECT WITH THE HOLY SPIRIT

---Come out of sin

One of the assignment of the devil is to *blind the mind of believers* from the truth of the gospel of Jesus Christ. *"In whom the god of this world hath blinded the minds of them which believe not, lest the light of the glorious gospel of Christ, who is the image of God, should shine unto them."* (2 Cor 4:4)

The devil desire to place believers under perpetual darkness. Unless we embrace the word of God, we remain a prey in the hand of the devil. For an example, if you are living an immoral life. A life defiled and filled with sin and gross immoralities Although God may warn you to come out such sin, God will leave you alone, for the most part.

---Come out of confusion

"For God is not the author of confusion, but of peace, as in all churches of the saints." **1 Cor 14:33**

Every time you are *confused* about *anything in life*. It is not by *the Holy Spirit. "For God is not the author of confusion."* Every time you cannot make a genuine decision concerning your future. It is from the pit of hell. To understand the voice of God, you must develop a sound mind. You must be decisive with a word of wisdom and understanding from the Lord.

---Practice Righteousness

From my scriptural studies and revelation, it takes righteousness to connect with the person of *the Holy Spirit*. It is written, *"Follow peace with all men, and holiness, without which no man shall see the Lord."* **Hebrew 12:14**

Unless we are determined to practice righteousness in our life, we will never connect with the Holy Ghost. It is the Holy Spirit who convicts anyone in life. It is written, *"And when he is come, he will reprove the world of sin, and of righteousness, and of judgment: Of sin, because they believe not on me; Of righteousness, because I go to my Father, and ye see me no more; Of judgment, because the prince of this world is judged."* **John 16:8-11**

"Howbeit when he, the Spirit of truth, is come, he will guide you into all truth: for he shall not speak of himself; but whatsoever he shall hear, that shall he speak: and he will shew you things to come." **John 16:13**

One good thing I know about the Holy Spirit is that He is a comforting spirit, who is never in a hurry. *"I will not leave you comfortless: I will come to you."* **John 14:18**.

What to do in times of difficulties hearing from God?

~Believe to hear from God

Unless you believe God wants to speak to you, you will not be able to recognize when he speaks to you. It is most likely that you won't hear or recognize His still, small voice. The truth is, you must connect to God before you can hear from Him, "David said, "O Lord, in the morning You will hear my voice; in the morning I will direct my prayer to You, and I will watch expectantly" (Ps. 5:3)

The Holy Spirit lives inside of you and speaks to you more often than you can imagine. Jesus said, "But the Counselor, the Holy Spirit, whom the Father will send in My name, will teach you everything and remind you of all that I told you" (John 14:26)

~Position yourself to hear from Him

Jesus Himself said, "My sheep hear my voice, and I know them, and they follow Me" (John 10:27) Our part is to position our hearts to hear His still, small voice, we must recognize any avenue God chooses to speak to us. In prayers, we experience His presence but in praise we enjoy His companionship. We must always position ourselves by creating an atmosphere of praise and worship.

We must therefore develop a relationship and fellowship with the person of the Holy Spirit.

~Fine-tune our hearing

There are times when *we hear from ourselves* and we claim we *heard from God*. Unless you *fine tune your hearing*, you *will either hear yourself, or hear others around you or hear the devil*. Often many *people talk to God without expecting to hear an answer*. Prayer is a dialogue and not a monologue. Ability *to hear* directly from God is a spiritual gift we all must covet. It is written, *"But covet earnestly the best gifts: and yet shew I unto you a more excellent way."* **1 Cor 12:30**

Whether in our natural relationships or our spiritual fellowship and relationship with God. We need a *sound hearing ear* to *hear from the Holy Spirit*. Jesus said, "He who has ears to hear, let him be listening and let him consider and perceive and comprehend by hearing" (Matt 13:9, AMP)

Solomon prayed that God would give him a hearing heart (1 Kings 3:9) Many translations say "understanding heart" in that verse but the Hebrew word translated "understanding" in that verse is shama, which translates to hear, understand, listen or obey. Pray that God will give you a hearing heart, then listen and obey.

~Fellowship with the Holy Spirit

In my own opinion, *without fellowship, there is no relationship with the Holy Spirit*. It is written, *"But if we walk in the light, as he is in the light, we have fellowship one with another, and the blood of Jesus Christ his Son cleanseth us from all sin. If we say that we have no sin, we deceive ourselves, and the truth is not in us. If we confess our sins, he is faithful and just to forgive us our sins, and to cleanse us from all unrighteousness."* **1 John 1:7-9**

Ability to hear from God is very vital in this end time. I do not know how others hear from Him, but God gave me special insight and deep word of revelation, I should call it to hear from Him. Although, some people call it world of knowledge, or word of wisdom. But I call it word of revelation.I have come to a level with my walk with the Holy Ghost that God honors the word that I speak. It is written, *"That confirmeth the word of his servant, and performeth the counsel of his messengers;"* **Isaiah 44:26**

I do not know of other ministers of God, but I hear from God daily per-time. Often God grants me deep insight to the things He is going to do. Three months before the Belgium terrorist attack, I heard it from the Lord and posted it on my face book wall. About five months before the Zika virus I heard it from the Lord and posted it on my Facebook wall. What am saying in effect is that there are men who genuinely hear from God. I am blessed to count myself among them.

Although knowing the word of God (the bible) protects us from deception and from falling into the trap of other evil voices or even following vain imaginations. If you seek God, you will hear His voice. We are told that God is spirit. If we must hear from the spirit we must be in the radar or frequency of the spirit.

It is written, *"Which things also we speak, not in the words which man's wisdom teacheth, but which the Holy Ghost teacheth; comparing spiritual things with spiritual. But the natural man receiveth not the things of the Spirit of God: for they are foolishness unto him: neither can he know them, because they are spiritually discerned."* **1 Cor 2:14-15**

CHAPTER 2

HOW TO HEAR FROM GOD

"Howbeit when he, the Spirit of truth, is come, he will guide you into all truth: for he shall not speak of himself; but whatsoever he shall hear, that shall he speak: and he will shew you things to come."
John 16:12

Unless you recognize *how to hear from God*, you will either *hear* yourself, or *hear* the enemy or *hear* your friends and co-workers. We are all spiritual being. Unless *you walk in the spirit*, you cannot *hear from God*. *"If we live in the Spirit, let us also walk in the Spirit."* **Gal 5:25**

The Holy scriptures have proven that God's voice is always consistent with His Word. It is written, *"Knowing this first, that no prophecy of the scripture is of any private interpretation. For the prophecy came not in old time by the will of man: but holy men of God spake as they were moved by the Holy Ghost."* **2 Peter 1:20-21**

Every passage of the Holy bible is directly from the mouth-piece of God. Every scripture always agrees with what the Lord is saying, even now to us all. *God's voice is soft*. Often *God speaks* to our *hearts through His Holy*

Spirit in an inaudible but in a convicting, and convincing manner. Every time you genuinely hear from God, no man can tell you otherwise. The Lord directs, reproves, instructs, and corrects in righteousness. It is written, ***"All scripture is given by inspiration of God, and is profitable for doctrine, for reproof, for correction, for instruction in righteousness."* 2 Timothy 3:16**

Whenever God speaks to us, it is either we *obey* or *disobey* Him. Most church folks may not share this truth but we either *willing and obeydience* or *refuse and rebel*. It is written, *"If ye be willing and obedient, ye shall eat the good of the land: But if ye refuse and rebel, ye shall be devoured with the sword: for the mouth of the Lord hath spoken it."* **Isaiah 1:19-20**

Most People who have ignored *the voice of God* have been devoured with the sword. Whenever you read second Samuel chapter one, King Saul will tell you more. Maybe God have called you into the ministry but you are still working as a nurse. I tell you unless you do the will of God you shall never experience total satisfaction in life. Although God will give us enough time to repent from our mistakes. It is always for a season or for within a time frame.

GOD SPEAKS TO US THROUGH OUR DREAMS

It is written, *"For God speaketh once, yea twice, yet man perceiveth it not. In a dream, in a vision of the night, when deep sleep falleth upon men, in slumberings upon the bed; Then he openeth the ears of men, and sealeth their instruction."* **Job 33:14-16**

Every now and then *God will give you a dream*. Often *God speaks through our dreams*. In *dreams*, we get a *revelation of warning, blessing, or a picture of the future*. Although there are *dreams* that frankly does not interpret into anything, but for the most part we should take *our dream life very serious.*

Whenever God gives you a *dream*, and you *remember it*, please *pay attention to it*. Pray to enforce *or to dismiss it* depending on *what was revealed to you*. But if you *dream* and you do not remember it, dismiss it *by praying aloud and in the spirit*.

Often most of us claim to know the interpretation of *any dream*. I like to submit to you that *dream* interpretation belongs to God. It is written, *"And Pharaoh said unto Joseph, I have dreamed a dream, and there is none that can interpret it: and I have heard say of thee, that thou canst understand a dream to interpret it. And Joseph answered Pharaoh, saying, It is not in me: God shall give Pharaoh an answer of peace."* **Genesis 41:15-16**

There are times when because of your retentive *memory bank*. Perhaps, all day you kept thinking of one *particular thing on your mind*. Quiet often by the end of the day, you have occupied and over loaded your *subconscious memory bank* with such thoughts. For the most part, Nine times out ten, you will definitely *dream about it*. Does that mean *God is speaking* to you about it? It is written, *"For a dream cometh through the multitude of business; and a fool's voice is known by multitude of words."* **Ecll 5:3**

Among the agents of the devil are familiar spirits whose assignment is to police, and harass the destinies of the saints *through our dreams. Familiar spirits are monitoring agents* assigned to interrupt our daily affairs in life. The devil will often try to *interrupt your dreams* with other *manipulating or torturing dreams* that appear scary and intimidating.

As a child of God, that should not scare you. Every time you get such revelation you should pray against it, and *bled the blood* of Jesus Christ. It is written, *"For the weapons of our warfare are not carnal, but mighty through God to the pulling down of strong holds; casting down imaginations, and every high thing that exalteth itself against the knowledge of God, and bringing into captivity every thought to the obedience of Christ;"* **2 Cor 10:4-5**

Warning Dreams

~God warned Pontus Pilate through His wife

It is written, *"When he was set down on the judgment seat, his wife sent unto him, saying, Have thou nothing to do with that just man: for I have suffered many things this day in a dream because of him."* **Matthew 27:19**

Every time your life is in a dangerous situation, God will give you a message of warning. Often we are very stubborn to obey the voice of God. Most folks do not like God's correction, especially if it comes with pain and hardship. *"Now no chastening for the present seemeth to be joyous, but grievous: nevertheless afterward it yieldeth the peaceable fruit of righteousness unto them which are exercised thereby."* **Hebrew 12:11**

It is written....

"And ye have forgotten the exhortation which speaketh unto you as unto children, My son, despise not thou the chastening of the Lord, nor faint when thou art rebuked of him: For whom the Lord loveth he chasteneth, and scourgeth every son whom he receiveth.

If ye endure chastening, God dealeth with you as with sons; for what son is he whom the father chasteneth not? But if ye be without chastisement, whereof all are partakers, then are ye bastards, and not sons. Furthermore we have had fathers of our flesh which corrected us, and we gave them reverence: shall we not much rather be in subjection unto the Father of spirits, and live?

For they verily for a few days chastened us after their own pleasure; but he for our profit, that we might be partakers of his holiness.

Now no chastening for the present seemeth to be joyous, but grievous: nevertheless afterward it yieldeth the peaceable fruit of righteousness unto them which are exercised thereby." **Hebrew 12:5-11**

~God warned Abimelech in a dream

Although King Abimelech wanted to commit sexual immoralities with sarah-Abraham's wife. God came *in a dream and warned him.* It is written, *"But God came to Abimelech in a dream by night, and said to him, Behold, thou art but a dead man, for the woman which thou hast taken; for she is a man's wife."* **Genesis 20:3**

God Warned Pharaoh King of Egypt in a dream

It is written, *"And Pharaoh said unto Joseph, I have dreamed a dream, and there is none that can interpret it: and I have heard say of thee, that thou canst understand a dream to interpret it. And Joseph answered Pharaoh, saying, It is not in me: God shall give Pharaoh an answer of peace."* **Genesis 41:15-16**

"For whom the Lord loveth he correcteth; even as a father the son in whom he delighteth." Proverb 3:12

---God warned Joseph---

"But when Herod was dead, behold, an angel of the Lord appeareth in a dream to Joseph in Egypt, Saying, Arise, and take the young child and his mother, and go into the land of Israel: for they are dead which sought the young child's life." **Matthew 2:19-20** Often God warns us in a dream in advance, of impending danger and trouble.

GOD SPEAKS THROUGH HIS PROPHET

It is written, *"Son of man, I have made thee a watchman unto the house of Israel: therefore hear the word at my mouth, and give them warning from me."* **Ezekiel 3:17**

"If there be a messenger with him, an interpreter, one among a thousand, to shew unto man his uprightness: Then he is gracious unto him, and saith, Deliver him from going down to the pit: I have found a ransom." Prophets are agents of God's solution for man's frustration in life. *"Surely the Lord God will do nothing, but he revealeth his secret unto his servants the prophets."* **Amos 3:7**

HOW DO I HEAR FROM GOD?

~Seek the face of God in Fasting

If you must *hear from God,* then you must be disciplined to fast as often as possible in life. Every time you fast and pray God speak and send divine helper. Daniel fasted and God sent Angel Gabriel. It is written, *"Then said he unto me, Fear not, Daniel: for from the first day that thou didst set thine heart to understand, and to chasten thyself before thy God, thy words were heard, and I am come for thy words."* **Daniel 10:12**

~Seek the face of God in Prayer

It is written, *"If my people, which are called by my name, shall humble themselves, and pray, and seek my face, and turn from their wicked ways; then will I hear from heaven, and will forgive their sin, and will heal their land."* **2 Chr 7:14**

If anyone lacks wisdom the bible says let him ask. If anyone must hear from God we must ask it in prayer. Every time you genuinely prays to God, angels intervenes in reciprocation to your prayers. Then said he unto me, Fear not, Daniel: for from the first day that thou didst set thine heart to understand, and to chasten thyself before thy God, thy words were heard, and I am come for thy words." **Daniel 10:12**

CONDITIONS TO RECEIVE THE HOLY SPIRIT

~REPENTANCE

Repent, and be baptized every one of you in the name of Jesus Christ for the remission of sins, and ye shall receive the gift of the Holy Ghost.

~BE BAPTIZED

"....be baptized every one of you in the name of Jesus Christ for the remission of sins, and ye shall receive the gift of the Holy Ghost." Acts 2:38

~CONFESS YOUR SIN

"If we confess our sins, he is faithful and just to forgive us our sins, and to cleanse us from all unrighteousness." 1 John 1:9

~ACKNOWLEDGEMENT

Acknowledge that you are a sinner and that Jesus Christ died for your sins. (Rom 3:23)

~BORN AGAIN

"Jesus answered and said unto him, verily, verily, I say unto thee, excpet a man be born again, he cannot see the kingdom of God." John 3:3

CONDITIONS FOR AQUAINTANCE OF THE HOLY SPIRT

WALKING IN THE SPIRIT

"This I say then, Walk in the Spirit, and ye shall not fulfil the lust of the flesh." Gal 5:17

FAITH

"We having the same spirit of faith, according as it is written, I believed, and therefore have I spoken; we also believe, and therefore speak." 2 Cor 4:13

WALK IN AGREEMENT

"Can two walk together, except they both agreed?" Amos 3:3

WALK IN LOVE

"And we have known and believed the love that God hath to us. God is love; and he that dwelleth in love dwelleth in God, and God in him." 1 John 4:16.

WALK IN TRUTH

"If the Son therefore shall make you free, ye shall be free indeed". John 8:32

WISDOM KEYS

— Every Productive Society is a society heading to the top.

— Millions of Nigerians run away from Nigeria, very few Nigerians stay in Nigeria.

— My decision to return Nigeria is the will of God for my life.

— My short coming in America after 18 years, trained me to be wise, to think, reflect and reason appropriately.

— If you train your mind to reason it will train your hands to earn money.

— It is absurd to use the money of the heathen to build the kingdom of the living God.

— Every Ministry reveals its agenda and goal either at the beginning or at the end. Be careful of your life it is your first Ministry.

— The average American mind is conditioned for a continual quest to get new things and (discard the former) and throw away old things.

— When I considered well, my BMW jeep became my initial deposit for the work of the ministry in Nigeria.

— Money will never fall from any tree.

— Everyone is waiting for you to change your mind until you change your thinking nothing changes around you.

— Multiple academic degrees in other discipline gave me the chance to think, reflect and reason.

— What so everyone are thinking and reflecting at the moment reveals you to the time and the now factor .

— All events and intents are the product of precise thought processes, accurate reason every event is designed for a designated timeline.

— Wisdom is your ability to think, to create and invent. If you can think wise enough you will come out of penury.

— The distance between you and success is your creative ability to think reason and reflect accurate.

— Success is the result of hard work, commitment resolve and determination learning from past mistakes and failing.

— If you organize your mind you have organized your life and destiny.

— There is a thin line between success and failure. If you look above and beyond you are on your way to success.

— Wealth is your ability to think, power is your ability to reason and success is your ability to be informed.

— If you can make use of your mind by thinking and reasoning God will make use of your life and destiny.

— Think and Be Great.

— Reflect, Reason, Think and Be Great.

— Famous people are born of woman.

— That you will make it is your intention; that you will survive is your resolve, that you will succeed with changes is your determination, personal efforts and hard work.

— No man was born a failure. Lack of vision is the end product of failure.

— Working with mental patients encourages and aspire me to be a productive observant and dedicated to my assignment.

— Successful people are not magicians, it is the will power combined with hard work, and determination and a resolve to succeed that make them succeed.

— In the unequivocal state of the mind, intention is not a location or a position it is the state of the mind.

— So many people think, that they think. The mind is used to think, reflect, and reason. You will remain blind with your eye open until you can see with your mind by thinking.

— There is no favoritism in accurate and precise calculation.

— Although knowledge is power, information is the key and gateway to a great future.

— It will take the hand of God to move the hand of man.

— With the backing of the great wise God, nothing will disconnect you from your inheritance.

— As long as you have wisdom and understanding of God, Satan and evil cannot manipulate your life and destiny.

— You have come this far by yourself judgment and decision you have made in the past, now lean and listen to God for another dimension of greatness.

— Great people are common people it is extra ordinary effort and the price of sacrifice that produces greatness.

— As a mental direct care worker I saw a great pastor and a motivational speaker within myself.

— Menial job does not reduce your self-worth, until you resolve to achieve greatness see greatness in all you do; you will never count in your community.

— The principle of Jesus will solve your gambling and addiction problems.

— The man of Jesus will lead you into heaven.

— Everyone have their self-appraisal and what they think about you. Until you discover yourself other opinion about you will alter the real you.

— Supervisors and directors are just a position in the chain of command in a work place. Never allow your supervisor hierarchy to alter your opinion about yourself.

— Everyone can come out of debt if they make up their mind.

— That I am not a decision maker at work does not diminish my contribution to my world.

— Although it appears like it was a poor decision to accept a direct care employment at a psychiatric hospital as I reflect of my nine years of experience, it became apparent that I have learnt and experienced enough for my next assignment in life.

— Self-encouragement and determination is a resolve of the heart.

— If you are determined to make a difference, and do the things that make a difference you will eventually make a difference.

— Good things do not come easy.

— Short cuts will cut your life short.

— Those who look ahead move ahead.

— Life is all about making an impact. In your life time strive to make an impact in your community.

— Make friends and connect with people who are moving ahead of you in life.

— If you can look around well you have come a long way in your life, made a lot of difference and realized a lot of success in life.

— If you are my old friend, hurry up to reach out to me before I become a stranger to you.

— Everything I am blessed with inspirations from God, that change my definition and interpretation of the world around me.

— I thought I was stagnant and lonely until I looked around and noticed my children running around and my wife cooking.

— At 40 I resigned my Job to seek the Lord forever.

— My ministry took a drastic rise to the top when the wisdom of God visited me with knowledge and understanding.

— You will be a better person, if you understand the characteristics of your personality – your mood swings, attitudes, and habits.

— It is the seed of love you sow into the heart of a child and a woman that you reap in due time.

— Love is not selfish, love share everything including the concealed secrets of the mind.

— As long as you have a prayer life and a bible; you will never feel lonely, rejected, and idle in the race of life.

— When good friends disconnect from you, let them go, they might have seen something new in a different direction.

— Confidence in yourself and in God is the only way to bring you out of captivity.

— Never train a child to waste his/her time.

— The mind is the greatest assets of a great future.

— You walk by common sense run by principles and fly by instruction.

— Those who fly in flight of life fly alone.

— Up in the air you are alone. No one can toll you accept the compass of knowledge and information.

— I have seen a towing vehicle I have seen a towing ship I have never seen a tolling airplane.

— I exercise my judgment and make a decision every minute of the day.

— Decisions are crucial, critical and vital with reference to your future.

— So many people wish for a great future. You can only work towards a great future.

— Your celebrity status began when you discovered your talent. What are you good at? Work at it with all commitment.

— Prayers will sustain you but the wisdom of God will prosper you.

— When I met Oyedepo, his teachings changed my perspective. But when I met Ibiyeomie; His teaching changed my perception.

— I will be successful in ministry if only I concentrate and focus my energy in the work of the ministry.

— It took the late Dr. Vincent Pearle Norman's book to open my mind towards kingdom success.

CHAPTER 3
PRAYER OF SALVATION

"Neither is there salvation in any other: for there is none other name under heaven given among men, whereby we must be saved."
Acts 4:12

The purpose of this book is to spread the word of God in print. The purpose is defeated if you do not accept the Lord as your personal savior and Lord over your life.

What must I do to determine my divine visitation?

To be saved we must be born again! The word says as many as received him, to them gave He power to become the sons of God. Even to them that believe on his name.

To qualify for divine visitation, do the following with sincerity—

1) Acknowledge that you are a sinner and that He died for you. (Romans 3:23)

2) Repent of your sins. (Acts 3:19, Luke 13:5, 2 Peter 3:9)

3) Believe in your heart that Jesus died for your sin. (Romans 10:10)

4) Confess Jesus as the Lord over your life. (Romans 10:10, Acts 2:21)

"Therefore if any man be in Christ, he is a new creature: old things are passed away; behold, all things are become new." 2 Cor 5:17

Now repeat this Prayer after me

Say Lord Jesus, I accept you today, as my Lord and my savior, forgive me of my sins wash me with your blood. Right now, I believe, I am sanctified, I am save, I am free, I am free from the Power of sin to serve the Lord Jesus. Thank you Lord for saving me. Amen.

Congratulations: You are now...

A BORN AGAIN CHRISTIAN.
Again I say to you—

CONGRATULATIONS!

I guarantee you! Watch the Spirit of God bear witness with your Spirit confirming His word with signs following. The word says The Spirit itself beareth witness with our spirit, that we are the children of God. Join a bible believing church or join us on our weekly and Sunday worship services at 343 Sanford Avenue, Newark, New Jersey, 07106.

Chapter 3   Prayer of Salvation

MIRACLE CARE OUTREACH

*"...But that the members should have
the same care one for another"*
1 Corinthians 12:25

We are all members of the body of Christ. Jesus commanded us to love our neighbor as ourselves. This includes caring for one another as a member of one body. True love is expressed in caring and giving. The word says for God so Love He gave….

Reach out to someone in need of Jesus, help someone in crisis find Christ. Look out and prove your love to Jesus by caring and inviting your friends and associates to find Jesus the Healer.

Invite your friends to our Home Care Cell Fellowship (Miracle chapel Intl Satellite fellowship) In the USA at 33 Schley Street, Newark, New Jersey, 07112. Home Care Cell fellowship Group meets every Tuesday at 6:00pm-7:00pm.

If you are in Nigeria—**MIRACLE OF GOD MINISTRIES**, aka **"MIRACLE CHAPEL INTL"** Mpama –Egbu-Owerri Imo state Nigeria.

LIFE IS NOT ALL ABOUT DURATION—
BUT ITS ALL ABOUT DONATION

What does the above statement mean?....

Life consists not in the accumulation of material wealth. (Luke 12:15) But it's all about liberality...meaning - what you can give and share with others. Proverb11:25. When you live for others—You live forever - because you out live your generation by the legacy you live behind after you depart into glory to be with the Lord. But when you live to yourself - you are reduced to self—you are easily forgotten when you die and depart in glory. Permit me to admonish you today to live your life to be a blessing to a soul connected to you today. I want you to know that so many souls are connected and looking up to you, and through you so many souls will be saved and rescued from destruction. Will you disciple someone today to find Jesus Christ?

As a genuine Christian; it is your duty to evangelize Jesus Christ to all you meet on your way. Jesus is still in the healing business-Jesus is still doing miracles from time of old to now. Therefore tell someone about Jesus Christ today, disciple and bring them to Church. (John 1:45) Philip findeth Nathanael....

Please to prove the sincerity of your love for God today; please become a soul winner. The dignity of your Christianity is hidden in your boldness to proclaim and evangelize Jesus Christ to all you meet on your way. There is a question mark on the integrity of your Christianity until you become a life soul winner. Invite someone to join us worship the Lord Jesus this coming Sunday. Amen.

MIRACLE OF GOD MINISTRIES

PILLARS OF THE COMMISSION

We Believe Preach and Practice the following:

1) We believe and preach Salvation to every living human being

2) We believe and preach Repentance and forgiveness of sins

3) We believe and preach the baptism of the Holy Spirit and Spiritual gifts

4) We believe and teach the Prosperity

5) We believe and preach Divine Healing and Miracles (Signs &Wonder)

6) We believe and preach Faith

7) We believe and proclaim the Power of God (Supernatural)

8) We believe and proclaim Praise& Worship to God

9) We believe and preach Wisdom

10) We believe and preach Holiness (Consecration)

11) We believe and preach Vision

12) We believe and teach the Word of God

13) We believe and teach Success

14) We believe and practice Prayer

15) We believe and teach Deliverance

These 15 stones form the Pillars of Our Commission. Become part of this church family and follow this great move of God.

MY HEART FELT PRAYER FOR YOU

It is my prayer that you testify today about the goodness of the Lord. I desire for you to have an encounter with our Lord Jesus Christ.

Now let me pray for you:

Father Lord, I pray and crave for you fresh Holy Spirit, to rekindle the life of this precious love one. In the Name of Jesus. I pray we develop a positive attitude in life against all obstacles facing us in the Name of Jesus. Amen

CONCLUSION

The voice of the Lord is powerful; the voice of the Lord is full of majesty. The voice of the Lord breaketh the cedars; yea, the Lord breaketh the cedars of Lebanon. (Psalms 29:4-5)

Unless we repent, we will never experience the genuine voice of God upon our lives. This book will remain a story to anyone who is not ready to make a decision for Jesus Christ. One man said if you failed to plan you have planned to fail in life. We want you to make plans to make heaven. The bible says "For God shall bring every work into judgment, with every secret thing, whether it be good, or whether it be evil." (Eccl 12:14) If you are a born again Christian; we like to encourage you in your Christian life. If you are not a born again Christian we can help you here receive genuine salvation.

What must I do to determine my divine visitation?

To determine divine visitation you must be born again! The word says as many as received him, to them gave He power to become the sons of God. Even to them that believe on his name.

To qualify for divine visitation, do the following with sincerity—

1) Acknowledge that you are a sinner and that He died for you. (Romans 3:23)

2) Repent of your sins. (Acts 3:19, Luke 13:5, 2 Peter 3:9)

3) Believe in your heart that Jesus died for your sin. (Romans 10:10)

4) Confess Jesus as the Lord over your life. (Romans 10:10, Acts 2:21)

"Therefore if any man be in Christ, he is a new creature: old things are passed away; behold, all things are become new." 2 Cor 5:17

Now repeat this Prayer after me

Say Lord Jesus, I accept you today, as my Lord and my savior, forgive me of my sins wash me with your blood. Right now, I believe, I am sanctified, I am save, I am free, I am free from the Power of sin to serve the Lord Jesus. Thank you Lord for saving me. Amen.

Congratulations: You are now...

A BORN AGAIN CHRISTIAN.
Again I say to you—

CONGRATULATIONS!

I guarantee you! Watch the Spirit of God bear witness with your Spirit confirming His word with signs following. The word says The Spirit itself beareth witness with our spirit, that we are the children of God. Join a bible believing church or join us on our weekly and Sunday worship services at 343 Sanford Avenue, Newark, New Jersey, 07106.

YOU MUST RECONGIZE THE VOICE OF GOD

Unless we turn to God in prayers and in intercession, we will miss our glorious future in life. God is the source of life. If we must align with divine plan with must turn to God in prayer and in thanksgiving in life. We must not miss our greatest opportunity of salvation in life.

It is written, *"If my people, which are called by my name, shall humble themselves, and pray, and seek my face, and turn from their wicked ways; then will I hear from heaven, and will forgive their sin, and will heal their land."* **2 Chronicle 7:14**

We are told, *"Woe unto him that striveth with his Maker! Let the potsherd strive with the potsherds of the earth. Shall the clay say to him that fashioneth it, What makest thou? or thy work, He hath no hands?"* **Isaiah 45:9**

We must return to God with a genuine repented hearted, for our salvation and for the favor of God upon our lives. If there is any constant prevailing challenges against your life, I pray in the Name of Jesus, let the power of God subdue the wicked one against your life even now in the Mighty Name of Jesus. Amen. You can call 973-393-8518 for immediate prayer right now. Amen.

CHAPTER 4
ABOUT THE AUTHOR

Rev Franklin N Abazie is the founding and Presiding Pastor of Miracle of God Ministries with headquarters in Newark, New Jersey USA and a branch church in Owerri- Imo State Nigeria. He is following the footsteps of one of his mentors, Oral Roberts (Healing Evangelist) of the blessed memory. The Lord passed Oral Roberts healing mantle two days before he went to be with the Lord at age 91 into the hand of healing evangelist-Rev Franklin N Abazie in a vision.

In all his services the Power and Presence of God is present to heal all in his audience. He is an ordained man of God with a Healing Ministry reviving the healing and miracle ministry of Jesus Christ of Nazareth.

Pastor Franklin N Abazie, is called by God with a unique mandate: **"THE MOMENT IS DUE TO IMPACT YOUR WORLD THROUGH THE REVIVAL OF THE HEALING & MIRACLE MINISTRY OF JESUS CHRIST OF NAZARETH**

"I AM SENDING YOU TO RESTORE HEALTH UNTO THEE AND I WILL HEAL

THEE OF THY WOUNDS. SAID THE LORD OF HOST"

Rev. Abazie is a gifted ardent Teacher of the word of God who operates also in the office of a Prophet, generating and attracting undeniable signs & wonders, special miracles and healings, with apostolic fireworks of the Holy Ghost. He is the founding and presiding senior Pastor of this fast growing Healing ministry. He has written over 86 inspirational, healing and transforming books covering almost all aspect of divine healing and life. He is happily married and blessed with children.

BOOKS BY REV FRANKLIN N ABAZIE

1) The Outcome of Faith
2) Understanding the secret of prevailing Prayers
3) Commanding Abundance
4) Understanding the secret of the man God uses
5) Activating my due Season
6) Overcoming Divine Verdicts
7) The Outcome of Divine Wisdom
8) Understanding God's Restoration Mandate
9) Walking in the Victory and Authority of the truth
10) Gods Covenant Exemption
11) Destiny Restoration Pillars
12) Provoking Acceptable Praise
13) Understanding Divine Judgment
14) Activating Angelic Re-enforcement
15) Provoking Un-Merited Favor
16) The Benefits of the Speaking faith
17) Understanding Divine Arrangement
18) Put your faith to work
19) Developing a positive attitude in life
20) The Power of Prevailing faith
21) Inexplicable faith
22) The intellectual components of Redemption.
23) Dominating Controlling Spirit
24) Understanding Divine Prosperity
25) Understanding the secret of the man God Uses
26) Retaining Your Inheritance
27) Never give up hope
28) Commanding Angelic Escorts
29) The winner's faith
30) Understanding Your Guardian Angels
31) Overcoming the Dominion of Sin
32) Understanding the Voice of God

33) The Outstanding benefits of the Anointing
34) The Audacity of the Blood of Jesus
35) Walking in the Reality of the Anointing
36) The Mystery of Divine supply
37) Understanding Your Harvest Season
38) Activating Your Success Buttons
39) Overcoming the forces of Darkness
40) Overcoming the devices of the devil
41) Overcoming Demonic agents
42) Overcoming the sorrows of failure
43) Rejecting the Sorrows of failure
44) Resisting the Sorrows of Poverty
45) The Restoring broken Marriages.
46) Redeeming Your Days
47) The force of Vision
48) Overcoming the forces of ignorance
49) Understanding the sacrifice of small beginning
50) The might of small beginning
51) Praying in the Spirit
52) Dominating controlling Spirits
53) Breaking the shackles of the curse of the law
54) Covenant keys to answered prayers
55) Wisdom for Signs & Wonders
56) Wisdom for generational Impact
57) Wisdom for Marriage Stability
58) Understanding the number of your Days
59) Enforcing Your Kingdom Rights
60) Escaping the traps of immoralities
61) Escaping the trap of Poverty
62) Accessing Biblical Prosperity
63) Accessing True Riches in Christ
64) Silencing the Voice of the Accuser
65) Overcoming the forces of oppositions
66) Quenching the voice of the avenger
67) Silencing demonic Prediction & Projection
68) Silencing Your Mocker

69) Understanding the Power of the Holy Ghost
70) Understanding the baptism of Power
71) The Mystery of the Blood of Jesus
72) Understanding the Mystery of Sanctification
73) Understanding the Power of Holiness
74) Praying in the spirit
75) Activating the Forces of Vengeance
76) Appreciating the Mystery of Restoration
77) Covenant Keys to Answered Prayers
78) Engaging the mystery of the blood
79) Commanding the Power of the Speaking faith
80) Uprooting the forces against Your Rising
81) Overcoming mere success syndrome
82) Understanding Divine Sentence
83) Understanding the Mystery of Praise
84) Understanding the Author of Faith
85) The Mystery of the finisher of faith
86) Where is your trust?

MIRACLE OF GOD MINISTRIES

*NIGERIA CRUSADE
2012*

MIRACLE OF GOD MINISTRIES

NIGERIA CRUSADE 2012

MIRACLE OF GOD MINISTRIES

NIGERIA CRUSADE 2012

www.ingramcontent.com/pod-product-compliance
Lightning Source LLC
Chambersburg PA
CBHW021157080526
44588CB00008B/390